LET'S GET REAL

ABOUT LIFE!

Really Choosing Eternal Rewards Over Eternal Punishments Is Where It's At!

AND

WHODUNIT

The Final Word On Criminal Minds According to Jesus Christ

A Modern Perspective

A Prophetic Pair of Books, By Courage

ISBN 978-1-64569-942-2 (paperback)
ISBN 978-1-64569-943-9 (digital)

Christian Faith Publishing, Inc.
832 Park Avenue
Meadville, PA 16335
www.christianfaithpublishing.com

Printed in the United States of America

LET'S GET REAL ABOUT LIFE!

Really Choosing Eternal Rewards Over Eternal
Punishments Is Where It's At!

Preface

In this Book, "LET'S GET REAL ABOUT LIFE!" unlike Justin Timberlake's song—Bringing *"Sexy Back"*, We are bringing sanity back! The following four (4) dichotomies are all-important to consider:

1) Good and evil
2) Right and wrong
3) Life and death
4) Heaven and hell.

Eternal Hell does not magically disappear because of John Lennon's song—*"Imagine"*. Hell is a real scientific fact, where sinners go, after death. One cannot pretend away Eternal Hell. Whoever chooses to spend Eternity in Hell is a fool!!

God and Jesus Christ want everyone on Earth, without exception, who are willing, to be Born Again, to enjoy all of the Heavenly Rewards!!

Both Good and evil can be great. You could be great in Good or great in evil. However, you don't want to be great in evil, because Eternal Hell follows death for all that choose to be evil and the worst Eternal Punishments, Justly, come upon those who are the greatest in evil!!

What is the use of being a person of vices, if such lives are sinful and wrong and always lead to death and Eternal Hell?

Freedom of speech is like a two-way street. If evil can try to lead people into Eternal Hell, We can try to lead people into the Eternal Heavenly Paradise!!

Is it worth it, for a small window of time in Eternity, to be a lying, hypocrite, who seeks to fool others, to lead a life of pseudo-hedonism, unto death and Eternal Hell?

Instead, when reading in this Book, **Chapter 2—Money, Success, and Prosperity**, see how easy it is to become <u>**enormously wealthy**</u>, to enjoy everything in **Chapter 1—Love, Sex, Marriage, and Family**, and while pleasing God and Jesus, you will enjoy the Eternal Heavenly Paradise that awaits!!

Sinful, pseudo-hedonistic, irresponsible, behavior has always occurred throughout Earth's History. To each his own. No one is questioning if one <u>could</u>, of one's own free will, lead such a foolish life. The real question is <u>should</u> one lead such a foolish life? A fool puts their own, selfish, sinful life first. Those who are Born Again put God and Jesus first and above all. This is how REALITY, scientifically, factually, really works, where free will is sacred. Therefore, being informed, everyone must choose between the two, above, simply doing the best one can!!

The masses, of Our Earth, pretend that sin is cool. Evil pretends that they are measuring up, but they are really measuring down. Such an individual is not cool, but a fool!! Whoever chooses to spend Eternity in Hell is a fool!!

Become Born Again through receiving the Grace of Jesus Christ. Don't follow John Lennon's siren song, "*Imagine*", being fooled, into Eternal Hell.

The wise, and those that are sane, understand that where a person spends Eternity, in a place of Eternal Rewards or in a place of Eternal Punishments, is what is all-important. Think about it. This is your real life. Let's get real about life! Do you really want to be fooled, by ignorant fools, unto death and Eternal Hell? No one has once ever taken any of their stolen idolatrous stuff with them into Eternal Hell. After death, it's all left behind.

Our Father God, Our Savior Jesus Christ, all of the Real Prophets and Saints, unanimously advise Us, all, to lead a life that is Good, doing what is Right, that will always lead Us to Eternal Life in Heaven!!

Who wants to be a foolish follower of an ignorant fool, suffering the, incomprehensible, agonies in Eternal Hell, forever and ever? This is your real life with your Righteous Virtuous Soul, your Self, who you really are, where you have been gifted by God with free will from your own Soul, to freely do as you please with your own life.

Get Real. Choose Jesus as your Lord and Savior. Repent of your sins and be Born Again, through receiving His Gift of Divine Grace!! It only takes your sincere merest intention. All of your sins will be forgiven and you will be Born Again, with Eternal life!!

If someone laughs and mocks at your Religion, that's their problem. Who would give up what is Most Precious to be played as a fool by demonic enemies, who seek to trick you into Eternal Hell, because their misery loves company?

Matthew 7.13–7.14: "Enter through the narrow gate; for the gate is wide and the road is easy that leads to destruction, and there are many who take it. For the gate is narrow and the road is hard that leads to life, and there are few who find it."

Be willing to stand alone. Be willing not to go along with the crowd. Don't be bullied into groupthink that seeks to get you in big trouble with sin, crime, or both. Instead, lead a Righteous, Virtuous Life, putting God and Jesus first and above all!!

"LET'S GET REAL ABOUT LIFE!" is broken up into Chapters that deals with what's really going on in Our World, helping Us all to always choose the right way to go in life, that leads to Heaven, as opposed to the wrong way, that leads to Hell.

You cannot have a personal relationship with Jesus if you don't know Him and don't obey His Teachings. When Mary Magdalene was caught in the act of committing adultery and was about to be stoned to death, Jesus saved her from the scribes and the Pharisees and said in John 8.11: "Go your way, and from now on do not sin again." Jesus did not say, as some pseudo-pastors say to their churches, to 'keep on sinning, because Jesus will keep on forgiving'. Only a moron encourages his church to sin, to be disobedient to the Teachings of Jesus Christ. Pseudo-pastors like them, greedily, take people's money to take them to Hell. They flatter their church members, trying to cheapen the Gift of Real Divine Grace and the Real

Salvation from Our Lord and Savior, Jesus Christ. There never was any Grace, in the first place, given to any hypocrite, who only pretended to believe in Jesus, in any church. Matthew 15.7–15.9: "You hypocrites! Isaiah prophesied rightly about you when he said: 'This people honors Me with their lips, but their hearts are far from Me; in vain do they worship Me, teaching human precepts as doctrines.'"

The masses pretend that they are going to Heaven, as their ploy, to pretend that all of their sinful activity is permissible and good. They mislead others, pretending that Hell is a four letter word taboo that should never be spoken.

In the hierarchy of love, it's easy to do what is right, with joy, and to not do what is wrong, out of one's love for the Beloved.

Luke 2.10–2.11: "I am bringing you good news of great joy for all the people: to you is born this day in the city of David a Savior, who is the Messiah, the Lord." It's easy to, meritoriously, choose a greater righteous pleasure over a smaller pleasure or over pain, out of one's love for the Beloved, without doing what is wrong.

My pseudonym is Courage, because it is only with the Virtue of Courage that one travels the Path of Justice.

Michael Douglas once said that—"Greed is good!" No, greed is evil, where, after death, the greedy go to Eternal Hell. Everyone chooses their own fate!! Travel the Courageous Path of Justice and choose Eternal Life, through Divine Grace!!

"LET'S GET REAL ABOUT LIFE!", a Virtuous Book of Quality, is intentionally written so that it can be easily read in one sitting. We hope all Readers will enjoy making good use of this Book throughout their lifetimes!

Love,

Courage

Contents

Chapter 1—Love, Sex, Marriage, and Family 11

Chapter 2—Money, Success, and Prosperity............................12

Chapter 3—Power..17

Chapter 4—Fame..19

Chapter 5—Purpose in Life, as Opposed to Frivolous Fun...........21

Chapter 6—Sacrifice and Serving a Just Cause Greater
              than Oneself..23

Chapter 7—Family, Friends, and Enemies...............................25

Chapter 8—Personal Problems..27

Chapter 9—Does Your Life Please God and Jesus? 29

Chapter 1—Love, Sex, Marriage, and Family

Hugh Hefner taught that males should be Playboys.

Jesus was and is a Celibate Virgin. Jesus Teaches in Matthew 22.30: "For in the Resurrection (in Heaven) they neither marry nor are given in marriage, but are like angels in Heaven." People should not go along, like sheep led to the slaughter, with their acculturation, which maximizes sins and sinful consequences from which they, Justly, cannot escape.

Who hasn't been subjected to pornography? The worst serial rapists/murderers all say that pornography was the #1 factor that fueled the fire of their criminal insanity that led to their monstrous lives. When will toxic masculinity begin to learn that females are entitled to their inalienable rights to have safe boundaries that protect the safety of their whole Selves—Soul, body, and stewardship?

No one should ever be abusively taunted nor coerced, who are faithfully waiting for their Soulmate, in order to enjoy a holy, love relationship, in marriage and with their entire family.

Matthew 13.41–13.43: "The Son of Man will send His angels, and they will collect out of His Kingdom all causes of sin and all evildoers, and they will throw them into the furnace of fire (Eternal Hell), where there will be weeping and gnashing of teeth. Then the Righteous will shine like the sun in the Kingdom of their Father. Let anyone with ears listen!" The Righteous have ears and listen and obey!!

Chapter 2—Money, Success, and Prosperity

The Author is not here to, wastefully, multiply words in an attempt to be quantitatively comprehensive, but rather to impart what might, qualitatively, be helpful to the Readers.

Money, like anything else, can be used for Good or for evil. If you desire to use money for Good, We, Righteous Forces and Principalities, advise the following:

Should you utilize "REALITY'S Law", which will now be briefly explained, if you have some surplus money saved, where you have an abundance to live within your means and to pay all of your bills, investing at your own risk, only invest in Equities that, consistently, are known to possess the highest percentage annualized profitability for the Shareholders!! All of the Equities, in the Diversified Portfolio, should exceed 50% profitability per year for the Shareholders!!

Allow Us to demonstrate how such compounded percentage profitability over the years, yields tremendous multiplication of your invested wealth. It's easy for anyone to buy Shares of Equities, without needing to pay any fee to some wealth management specialist, who usually picks less than average profitable equities, while depleting the compounded percentage profitability, charging quarterly fees on the Value of the entire Portfolio. Once you know, for certain, confirmed by a trusted Financial Expert, such as readily found on Our Media, your chosen Equities, the top most consistently profitable, the best of the best, observe, over the years, how rich you will become!! For example, let's assume a 50% annualized profitability for the Shareholders, over a thirty (30) year time frame, as follows: For example, let's observe the growth of your investments when starting with $30 thousand or when starting with $1 million:

$30 thousand + 50% profit, after one year = $45 thousand.
$1 million + 50% profit, after one year = $1.5 million.

	Starting with $30 thousand	Starting with $1 million
Year 1:	$45,000	$1.5 million
Year 2:	$67,500	$2.25 million
Year 3:	$101,250	$3.375 million
Year 4:	$151,875	$5.0625 million
Year 5:	$227,812.5	$7.59375 million
Year 6:	$341,718.75	$11.390625 million
Year 7:	$512,578.12	$17.085937 million
Year 8:	$768,867.18	$25.628905 million
Year 9:	$1,153,300.7	$38.443357 million
Year 10:	$1,729,951	$57.665035 million
Year 11:	$2,594,926.5	$86.497552 million
Year 12:	$3,892,389.7	$129.74632 million
Year 13:	$5,838,584.5	$194.61948 million
Year 14:	$8,757,876.7	$291.92922 million
Year 15:	$13,136,815	$437.89383 million
Year 16:	$19,705,222	$656.84074 million
Year 17:	$29,557,833	$985.26111 million
Year 18:	$44,336,749	$1.4778916 billion
Year 19:	$66,505,123	$2.2168374 billion
Year 20:	$99,757,684	$3.3252561 billion
Year 21:	$149.63652 million	$4.9878841 billion
Year 22:	$224.45478 million	$7.4818261 billion
Year 23:	$336.68217 million	$11.222739 billion
Year 24:	$505.02325 million	$16.834108 billion
Year 25:	$757.53487 million	$25.251162 billion

	Starting with $30 thousand	Starting with $1 million
Year 26:	$1.1363023 billion	$37.876743 billion
Year 27:	$1.17044534 billion	$56.815114 billion
Year 28:	$2.5566801 billion	$85.222671 billion
Year 29:	$3.8350201 billion	$127.834 billion
Year 30:	$5.7525301 billion	$191.751 billion

So, in this example, after 30 years of investing, should you utilize "REALITY'S Law", above, then:

1) A one-time investment of $30,000 would make you a Billionaire within 26 years!!
2) A one-time investment of $1 million would make you richer than Jeff Bezos is now, the current richest man in Earth's History, within 30 years!!

REALITY'S Law should be utilized to bring World Peace, Prosperity, and Justice for all!!

As you can see, the more that extremely successful Investors multiply, globally, through utilizing REALITY'S Law, the more the World will be able to solve all global problems, as much as possible, without constraint.

$5.7525301 billion, above, divided by $30,000 = 191,751 times the original investment.

$191.751 billion, above, divided by $1 million = 191,751 times the original investment.

The math never lies, whether you invest, in this example, $30,000 or $1 million, in either instance, you will earn, as an Investor or Shareholder, 191,751 times your one-time investment after 30 years!!

After 10, 20, or 30 years of investment, how much money did the investor earn, on the average per year, for the original $30,000 investment or for the original $1 million investment?

If the investor sold all of the shares in the $30,000 portfolio, after 10, 20, or 30 years, the investor would have earned, on the average per year, the following:

After 10 years: $172,995.10 per year, for each of the 10 years.
After 20 years: $4,987,884.20 per year, for each of the 20 years.
After 30 years: $191.751 million per year, for each of the 30 years.

So we see how a $30,000 investment, in this example, pays $191.751 million per year, for each of the 30 years. Who wouldn't want that? You could, easily, make that happen for yourself. Thank God and Jesus for the Blessings of the Gospel!!

If the investor sold all of the shares in the $1 million portfolio, after 10, 20, or 30 years, the investor would have earned, on the average per year, the following:

After 10 years: $5.7665035 million per year, for each of the 10 years.
After 20 years: $166.2628 million per year, for each of the 20 years.
After 30 years: $6.3917 billion per year, for each of the 30 years.

So, We see how a $1 million investment, in this example, pays $6.3917 billion per year, for each of the 30 years. Who wouldn't want that? You could, easily, make that happen for yourself. Thank God and Jesus for the Blessings of the Gospel, whether you could save, in the above example, $30,000 or $1 million, to wisely invest!!

As you can see, the math never lies. So, We see how your money can work for you, when intelligently invested, as a skillful steward. This money can be used to pay for everything in **Chapter 1—Love, Sex, Marriage, and Family**. God and Jesus are Good!!

Of course, if the Equities Markets, for your chosen investments, yielded average annualized percentage profits that were more or less than the 50%, in the above example, then the resulting numerics would be exactly more or less than above, for that specific average annualized percentage of profits!!

Whenever the Equities Markets become volatile and bearish, you could sell all of your Shares of Equities, keeping your money safe in the Investment Bank Deposit Program, earning Interest on your money, waiting until it's safe to buy on the dip, going all in to enjoy the booming, bullish, highly profitable, Markets, again, as soon as it's safe to invest!! There are, almost always, many Equities that have more than 50% annualized profitability for the Shareholders to choose from, in which to invest!!

John 8.31–8.32: "Then Jesus said to the Jews who had believed in Him, 'If you continue in My word, you are truly My disciples; and you will know the Truth, and the Truth will make you free.'"

The Author has always been poor, always explaining the Gospel for free and at his own expense, never receiving even a penny, hence, I never had money for, the above, investments. The first time that I may earn money explaining the Gospel is through, the wonderful and blessed, Christian Faith Publishing.

Chapter 3—Power

When I began my freshman year at my university, a fellow student, that I just met, asked me, with a mocking laugh—"You're not going to take a *poli sci* class are you?" I didn't know what that meant, so I asked someone and he explained that the student was talking about a political science class. Especially, because of his mocking laugh at me, I never really thought about taking a course in political science. Evil forces and principalities wanted to keep me ignorant about such things.

Since then, I learned that throughout Earth's History, political science was used by people who sought power, including to possess command and influence over the law, over the means of production, over the military and police, and over vast numbers of people and resources on Earth, etc. A little thing like that, I say sarcastically!!

Augustus Caesar held power over the Roman Empire and over Jesus Christ, crucifying Him, when instigated by the, pseudo-religionist, Sanhedrin, including Caiaphas, etc., out of their, insatiable, lust for power, money, and for all of the stolen rewards of life!!

The kleptocratic bullies, throughout Earth's History, have always, violently, owned and controlled the major unjust happenings on Earth, cursing Our World. The more they steal the fruits of everyone's labor, selfishly, idolatrously, pretending that they are above God, Christ, the Just Law, etc., the more superior they pretend to be.

They have always pretended, trying to make everyone into naive, patsies, and fools, that they are the most superior on Earth. About them, Jesus Teaches in Matthew 19.24: "Again I tell you, it is easier for a camel to go through the eye of a needle than for someone who is rich to enter the Kingdom of God." If a sinner's greed wants to contest the words of Jesus Christ, pretending that they know better than Him, fine. Let them take their chances, after death, and they'll find out. There were kleptocratic pseudo-religionists in the time of Jesus and there are kleptocratic pseudo-religionists today. They take people's money to take them to Hell, pretending that their hypocritical promises can contest Matthew 19.24, above.

When it comes to Power, We advise to always put God and Christ first and above all others in your life, as Commanded by God and Jesus!! Matthew 22.37–22.38: "He said to him, 'You shall love the Lord your God with all your heart, and with all your Soul, and with all your mind.' This is the greatest and first Commandment."

Chapter 4—Fame

The Beatles (the rock band) once bragged, falsely, that they were more popular than Jesus Christ. Do the Beatles really want to, narcissistically, compare themselves to Jesus Christ, thinking that they will escape Heavenly Judgment?

Why do the demons pretend that people are all equals, like in a democracy where everyone has an equal vote, as if there were no Justly merited and Justly anti-merited hierarchy of human beings? Should the vote of Jesus Christ be equal to a demon's vote? Obviously not!!

No. We may be standing on flat ground together, but We are not all equals, as if standing on a horizontal line with no hierarchy. While We are all Created in the Image of God, with Soul, Free Will, and Intelligence, how each of Us actualizes Our potential, for Good or for evil, of Our own free will, Justly determines Our real hierarchy, as time marches on.

While Heavenly Judgment is Perfectly Just, We are all being judged, unjustly, by a man-made, rigged system, like on an upside-down 'vertical number line', where Our Justly Merited Hierarchy is unjustly judged to be the opposite of Our Real and Just Hierarchy under God and Christ!! Some people are flattered and rewarded unjustly and others are slandered and punished unjustly.

Due to this man-made, rigged system, Augustus Caesar, as a bully, violently, unjustly, pretended that he was god and king. Caiaphas, as a bully, violently, unjustly, pretended that he was the high priest. The Lamb of God Who takest away the sins of the world, Our Lord and Savior, Jesus Christ, was, in a man-made, rigged system, and was unjustly judged to be slandered and crucified by almost all of the Romans and the Jews, at the time. The rigged system has only gotten worse, every year, for over 2,000 years, but evil is here to fool Our World.

Jesus Christ was the Real Divine, God, King, and High Priest, but Caesar and Caiaphas unjustly stole that honor for themselves. They became, after death, the first who shall finish last, while Jesus became the last who shall finish first. Their sinful, idolatrous, selfishness led to their deaths into Eternal Hell, but Jesus prepared the way, for all who would truly become Born Again, to enjoy His Heavenly Kingdom!!

The demons have always pretended that they are the top, like in an upside-down 'vertical number line', the most innocent, right, and superior, while pretending that the Righteous are the bottom, the most guilty, wrong, and inferior. Evil has, always, in the delusional anti-REALITY in which they all, narcissistically, live, had this lying, anti-rational propaganda. In spite of evil taboos, "to shut up and just go along with evil", We are explaining, in this Book, past, present, and future, what is really happening between Good and evil.

No, the Righteous have always really been the top, like in a right side up 'vertical number line', with plus above the zero and minus beneath the zero, the most innocent, right and superior, while the demons have always been the bottom, the most guilty, wrong, and inferior!! When the demons make their, narcissistic, false claims, they have always used these claims to further claim credit for what the Righteous have Justly merited to do, while stealing the fruits of the labor from the Righteous and wicked alike. The demons, as bullies, then back up their claims with military and police, like Maduro in Venezuela, like the Castros of Cuba, like Kim Jong-Un of N. Korea, like Putin of Russia, like Adolf Hitler of Nazi Germany, and like Augustus Caesar of the Roman Empire!! And their evil curses continue, on Earth, today.

The Final Coming will have Real Fame, Divine Fame, where His True Fame will be unanimous and uncontested, as He fulfills the Prophecy in Matthew 6.10: "Your Kingdom come. Your Will be done, on Earth as it is in Heaven." There will be no more sin, no more injustice, no more suffering, no more disease, and no more death. There will be Miraculous Healing, Miraculous Rejuvenation to any desirable age, Eternal Life of Joy, Peace, Prosperity, and Love for All, in The Kingdom of Heaven on Earth!!

Chapter 5—Purpose in Life, as Opposed to Frivolous Fun

When I was little, I used to think that life was about having friends, playing, and having fun together. Thank God that I grew up and realized the seriousness of the situation that We are all in, here in life, in REALITY!! Heaven and Hell, all of the Rewards and all of the Punishments, await, based on free will is sacred, for all competing life in REALITY!

By no means are We in any way, at all, against anyone who is really Born Again. We are 100% for everyone who are truly Born Again, without exception. So, please, if you really are Born Again, then this Book is not contesting you in any way, at all. For example, even before the Grace of Jesus, King Solomon and Job were, praiseworthy, Righteous, rich males. We are all competing for the rewards and punishments, in an unjust system of gender inequality, wealth inequality, etc. Nowadays, rich males are, generally, in power, throughout Our Earth and that is how it's always been throughout History. All of the inherited violent leverages and momentums are on the side of rich males. This is why Jesus Taught in Matthew 19.24, above, about the unjust greed of rich males, where the rich get richer and the poor get poorer. Even in America today, We see how U.S. deficit indebtedness, at more than $22 Trillion, and unfunded liabilities, at more than $200 Trillion, caused by the rich males with their violent power, violent ownership, and violent control, keep increasing the above, pretending that their, increasingly, indebted *'slaves'* are inferior and just keep becoming more indebted to them. Just look at the U.S. Debt Clock!! The kleptocratic males steal almost all of the profits, unjustly, from the fruits of everyone's labor, yet they divide indebtedness equally, unjustly, against the rest of Us.

The purpose in life of Righteous Forces and Principalities has always been to restore Just Divine Order through Divine Grace, Divine Justice, and the perfect balance of all of the other Divine Virtues, such as Love, Truth, Mercy, Compassion, Kindness, Courage, Etc. All of the rewards and punishments should be Justly restored, where the Righteous become Justly rewarded and the wicked become Justly punished, not the other way around, unjustly. Throughout Earth's History, evil rich male kings have always unjustly persecuted the Righteous, while stealing the rewards of evil temptation for themselves, pretending that they are the divine god and divine king. Today, pseudo-religionists, of every kind, that give hypocritical lip service to God and to the Leaders of the World Religions, cloud the issues above with propaganda. These pseudo-religionist rich males, like Caiaphas in the time of Jesus, have settled for the stolen rewards of evil temptation, while giving hypocritical lip service to God and Christ, only sometimes pretending that they, the pseudo-religionists, are legitimate Gods and Kings.

You can lead a horse to water, but you can't make it drink. If people want to deny all of the above, free will is sacred, but the hypocritical teachings of the pseudo-religionists will save no one after death, including the, greedy, inheritors of the kleptocratic pseudo-religionists.

Justice is rewards for the Righteous and punishments for the wicked. When the rich males, as previously stated, We are not presuming all of them to be wicked, violently, unjustly, steal the rewards and unjustly punish the Righteous, this rigged unjust system will be overturned, like the tables of the money changers in the Holy Temple by Jesus, by the Final Coming, restoring Divine Order Justly in the Kingdom of Heaven on Earth!! This is not crazy, nor fiction, nor a fairy tale, as some suppose, but rather, this is Scriptural Prophecy, that is guaranteed to become True, until The Kingdom of Heaven on Earth is Manifest!!

Chapter 6—Sacrifice and Serving a Just Cause Greater than Oneself

It is noble and good to sacrifice and to serve a just cause greater than oneself. When individuals accomplish the above, putting the sins of the idolatry of selfishness behind them, they are emulating the greatest of all men, like Abraham, Moses, and Jesus.

When Abraham was willing to sacrifice his son Isaac, in obedience to the Commandment of God, waiting for 100 years for Isaac's birth, where Sarah waited till she was 90 years old before giving birth to their beloved son, Isaac, imagine the immense level of sacrifice, putting the Just Cause of God first, above themselves.

Genesis 22.11–22.12: "But the angel of the Lord called to him from Heaven, and said, 'Abraham, Abraham!' And he said, 'Here I am.' He said, 'Do not lay your hand on the boy or do anything to him; for now I know that you fear God, since you have not withheld your son, your only son, from Me.'"

When Moses experienced the Burning Bush and was willing to return to Egypt, unjustly convicted of murder by the evil Pharaoh and banished from Egypt under the penalty of death, imagine the immense level of sacrifice, putting the Just Cause of God first, above himself.

Exodus 3.4–3.8: "When the Lord saw that he had turned aside to see, God called to him out of the Bush, 'Moses, Moses!' And he said, 'Here I am.' Then He said, 'Come no closer! Remove the sandals from your feet, for the place on which you are standing is holy ground.' He said further, 'I am the God of your father, the God of Abraham, the God of Isaac, and the God of Jacob.' And Moses hid his face, for he was afraid to look at God. Then the Lord said, 'I have observed the misery of My people who are in Egypt; I have heard

23

their cry on account of their taskmasters. Indeed, I know their sufferings, and I have come down to deliver them from the Egyptians, and to bring them up out of that land to a good and broad land, a land flowing with milk and honey…'"

When Jesus was willing to be crucified, in obedience to the Commandment of God, imagine the immense level of sacrifice, taking on all of Our sins, with His Divine Courage, Divine Love, Divine Forgiveness, and Divine Grace, in order that We should become Born Again to serve Our Father God and His only begotten Son, Jesus, putting the Just Cause of God, above Himself.

Matthew 27.46–27.54: "And about three o'clock Jesus cried with a loud voice, 'Eli, Eli, lema sabachthani?' that is, 'My God, My God, why have You forsaken Me?' When some of the bystanders heard it, they said, 'This man is calling for Elijah.' At once one of them ran and got a sponge, filled it with sour wine, put it on a stick, and gave it to Him to drink. But the others said, 'Wait, let's see whether Elijah will come to save Him.' Then Jesus cried again with a loud voice and breathed His last. At that moment the curtain of the Temple was torn in two, from top to bottom. The earth shook, and the rocks were split. The tombs also were opened, and many bodies of the saints who had fallen asleep were raised. After His Resurrection they came out of the tombs and entered the Holy City and appeared to many. Now when the centurion and those with him, who were keeping watch over Jesus, saw the earthquake and what took place, they were terrified and said, 'Truly this man was God's Son!'"

Chapter 7—Family, Friends, and Enemies

Who are one's family, friends, and enemies?

Mark 3.31–3.35: "Then His mother and His brothers came; and standing outside, they sent to Him and called Him. A crowd was sitting around Him; and they said to Him, 'Your mother and Your brothers and sisters are outside, asking for You.' And He replied, 'Who are My mother and My brothers?' And looking at those who sat around Him, He said, 'Here are My mother and My brothers! Whoever does the will of God is My brother and sister and mother.'"

Although the Popes don't like to admit that the Virgin Mary, after the Immaculate Conception and Birth of Jesus, was raped and had evil progeny, of course, to no fault of her own, Jesus was quite aware. So, from the above, We understand the difference between those who are sincerely Born Again and those who are not yet Born Again. Some of those who are not yet Born Again may even reveal themselves to you, as your enemies.

Regarding enemies, it is vital not to be naive. Never be afraid to be alone. When you are certain that such individuals are your enemies, always make sure that your boundaries are securely established and that your, offensive and defensive, battle strategies are in place. 'Close the door' of doubt on your past notions about your enemies, having nothing to do with them. Make certain that they have no way of contacting you, let alone any way to approach you. Make certain that you feel 100% safe and secure from them and that you have no fear of any, potential, threats or coercion from them. Better safe than sorry!

Matthew 10.35–10.39: "For I have come to set a man against his father, and a daughter against her mother, and a daughter-in-law against her mother-in-law; and one's foes will be members of one's own household. Whoever loves father or mother more than Me is not worthy of Me; and whoever loves son or daughter more than Me is not worthy of Me; and whoever does not take up the cross and follow Me is not worthy of Me. Those who find their life will lose it, and those who lose their life for My sake will find it."

What do the Judgments of Jesus, above, mean? What does "not worthy of Me" mean? He is explaining that they have not sincerely received His Grace to become Born Again, putting their idols (false gods) in their lives first and above Him. They are disobedient to His Teachings and even if they would give hypocritical lip service to Him, like Judas Iscariot, they are not trustworthy. When almost everyone on Earth pretend to be Righteous and going to Heaven after death, no one should be fooled by any of these pseudo-religionists.

Chapter 8—Personal Problems

When someone has personal problems, it would be wise to surround oneself with Born Again, trustworthy, people, who have their lives together, who are good role models, as stewards. Such individuals will be far superior to professionals, who are often uncaring and greedy, keeping their customers coming back. These role models, above, will help to refer you to, any and all, professionals, when needed, who are worthy and most excellent in offering you their services.

In obedience to God and Christ, We only offer you Our best advice, however, you are always responsible for your own actions that you choose of your own free will.

Personal problems need to be clearly defined. One always needs to be certain to clearly understand and to know for certain, without any doubt, exactly what one's personal problems really are, before one can ascertain the solutions to one's personal problems. Most of the solution to all personal problems is, simply, not to have any delusions nor denial about such problems.

One should live a life of "everything in moderation", always putting God and Christ first and above all. You will not find real happiness, in your lifetime nor after death, through insatiable lust for money, nor for any of the idolatrous stolen rewards.

Don't have any addictions and learn to enjoy transcendental consciousness. Take good care of Our Earth and the Earth will take good care of Us.

Let your diet be very low in saturated fats, trans-fats, and sugar. Keep your cholesterol low, where HDL is maximized and LDL is minimized. Enjoy lots of organic vegetables, fruits, phytonutrients, and plant-based protein powdered smoothies. Get plenty of exercise. Be happy and with character, principles, and honorability, serve a

Just Purpose in Life!! Work, living within your means, where you serve others in all-positive ways.

Nip real problems in the bud. Don't let them get worse. Solve them as soon as possible, putting them behind you. Be detached and forgiving about any stigmatization that took place and move on with your life in Righteous, happy, and successful ways.

Chapter 9—Does Your Life Please God and Jesus?

Ask yourself if your life really pleases God and Jesus? This is your real, one and only, life, before you die and go to a place of Eternal Rewards or Eternal Punishments!! It is the most important question you need to ask yourself. Are you really Born Again or not?

I knew someone and he said to me that he never had any "big deal" experience when he became born again nor when he was baptized. He said that he believes in Charles Darwin's theory of evolution, more than he believes in God, as Creator, or in Jesus, as Savior. He saw himself as a saint and prophet, greater than Job, in the delusional anti-REALITY in which he lived.

It is extremely common that people have doubts, delusions, and denials about their Salvation. There is no place for doubt, delusion, nor denial, at all, regarding the certainty that is needed about one's own Salvation!!

Kleptocratic pseudo-religionist leaders abound who, narcissistically and disobediently, proclaim, against the Commandments of God and Jesus that they are Pastors, Rabbis, Father/Priests, Bishops, Popes, etc.

Matthew 23.8–23.10: "But you are not to be called rabbi for you have one Teacher, and you are all students. And call no one your father on Earth, for you have one Father—the one in Heaven. Nor are you to be called instructors, for you have one Instructor, the Messiah."

Please, put your own Salvation above their pseudo-religionist lust to be flattered with titles of honor. Put God and Christ first and above all others in your life!! Do your very best to repent of your sins and to be Born Again through the Divine Grace of Our Lord and Savior, Jesus Christ!!

Love,

Courage

WHODUNIT

The Final Word on Criminal Minds
According to Jesus Christ

A Modern Perspective

Preface

"Whodunit" answers all of the questions about who is behind all criminal activity and behind all evil enemies of all Wars.

"Whodunit", more importantly, answers all of the questions about who is behind all Meritorious and Virtuous activity, until the War between Good and evil is Won, in fulfillment of Prophecy!!

You must decide if you will obey the Just Commandments of the Laws of God and Christ or be a foolish follower of the evil archenemy of all life!!

If you still believe in Santa coming down the chimney with gifts or prefer not to hear the Truth, then this Book is not for you.

Naiveté, cowardliness, and fear need to be put behind you when understanding about The Real Whole Just Truth of the Matter, getting real about Good and evil and about the criminally insane. "Whodunit" reveals the specific source of all criminal minds.

Should you turn the page, no harm can be done, but you will be, greatly, more prepared to deal with all of life's real injustices and problems and become more certain of your own Salvation.

My pseudonym is Courage, because it is only with the Virtue of Courage that one travels the Path of Justice.

"Whodunit", a Virtuous Book of Quality, is intentionally written so that it can be easily read in one sitting. We hope all Readers will enjoy making good use of this Book throughout their lifetimes!

All life has righteous, virtuous Souls with free will. All life of their own free wills are 100% responsible for who they are and for what they do, for Good or for evil.

There is a Justly merited hierarchy of Good stewards and a Justly anti-merited hierarchy of evil stewards in REALITY, of their own free wills.

The fainthearted may want to pretend to live in a World where there is no danger, but evil violent injustice can be taken to an extreme in the minds of the criminally insane.

With all of Earth's evil, in all of Earth's History, it should be understood that there is a reason and a source for that evil.

No, it's not an accident, a coincidence, nor a random chance, but there is a violently evil, criminally insane, monster that is 100% responsible for intentionally bringing about, directly and indirectly, the worst in others. He, constantly and ubiquitously, violently, and at all levels of Being, tries to get others to, maximally, do sin and crime. In scientific investigation, it is important to be open-minded about the source and root of all evil. Evil forces and principalities wants everyone to be naive, patsies, and fools, thereby maximizing their evil effectiveness and victory when violently bullying and attacking all life. Evil seeks to extort more violent leverages and momentums to bring about the extinction of all life.

Grow up and get real and don't let evil violent injustice win.

Only by defining the problem and the solution correctly, by not underestimating the evil enemy, can one hope to be the victor in the, Constant, Eternal War between Good and evil.

Evil wants people to laugh away their lives on frivolous lifestyles, until it's too late, until they die and go to Eternal Hell. Fools live a life of hypocritical lies and then die into Eternal Hell. Who thinks that it's funny being fooled by evil when all of the Eternal Rewards and Eternal Punishments are dependent on not being fooled?!!

In Earth's History, there never has been an evil global dictator. There have been diverse levels of evil empires, but in the War between Good and evil, no evil dictator has ever been able to take over the entire Earth, thank God. The root and source of all evil wants to get some human being to succeed to become an evil global dictator, where he has a monopoly on power, where the balance of power is such that he has no real competitors. With a monopoly on evil violent injustice, this source of all evil wants him to murder all of his competitors and eventually to murder everyone who may contest his evil will.

Why doesn't this source of all evil do it himself?

Out of fear, it's easy to nervously laugh and to have delusion and denial, stubbornly trying to escape the true answer to the above question.

The answer is that this source of all evil has his capabilities and his limitations and cannot do it himself.

Why not?

The answer is not found by thinking inside the box. In Earth's History, the answer is only now being revealed in this Book for the very first time.

When Our Father God Created all life in Our Vast Creation, He had competitors who coveted the Superiority of Our Creation, who wanted to violently imperialize Our Creation.

So, Our Father God protected Our entire Creation by surrounding it with Impenetrable Invincible Protective Energy.

Let Us realize the Truth about microcosmicity and macrocosmicity. Things happen, based on the free will of all life, in a small-time or in a big-time way. While there may be violent disputes in a household, at the same time, there may be violent crime in a municipality. At the same time, there may even be a violent War between Nations.

While some people don't know how to cope with personal problems, Our Father God knew that people, in general, might have trouble coping with inter-creational War! The source of all evil wants you to be small-minded and to underestimate the enemy of evil. In his evil divide and conquer, he wants you to mock, laugh at, slander, and attack the Author.

Evil happens on all levels. Just like it's possible that there are evil microscopic bacteria, there are also evil creators with evil creations. Our Father God has taken care of this problem when surrounding Our entire Creation with Impenetrable Invincible Protective Energy!

While Star Trek is science fiction, an evil creator, literally, has prioritized his Creational Economy for inter-creational War, led by his evil artificial intelligent monster machine. His evil space warships and their weapons, with advanced technology and miracles can travel almost infinitely faster than the speed of light. However, it is literally impossible for any of these enemy space warships to get through the Impenetrable Invincible Protective Energy of Our Father God, the Most Powerful of all Creators!!

However, the sensors of these evil enemy space warships, but never the warships themselves, can partially get through the above Energy, as invisible energy with information content, constantly ubiquitously attacking all life in Our Creation and at all levels of Being. The sensors cannot attack the subtle free will intentions from the Souls of all life, because the violent physical is powerless against the Spiritual Souls and its Subtle Spiritual Free Wills. However, the sensors can violently put thoughts into people's heads, while trying to convince them that it's their thoughts, but it's all coming from the evil enemy, not from Us, at all. Be detached and simply continue with your purposeful life. The evil attack is relentless, should a person become aware and no longer be in denial.

In War, part of readiness is to know the Truth about your enemies. If the Reader is not ready to hear about atrocities of War, please
skip this part and continue three (3) paragraphs, below, starting
with "That is why Augustus Caesar". That evil alien creator, in his
War against Our Earth, with his depraved libido, desperately seeks,
through his proxies, to violently rape, sodomize, beastial creatures
and human beings. He wants to bring about the extinction of all
life, except for the beastial creatures and the human males, for the
evil depravities of beastiality and male '*homo*' (there is nothing sexual
about rape) rape. If you choose to not believe in the above, God bless
you, but this is part of the evil, hidden, secret, mystical REALITY in
which We all live.

By knowing who are the most superior, God and Jesus, and who
are the most inferior, that evil creator and his monster machine, you
know, clearly, Who you should be for and who you should be against.
You, clearly, understand the greatest in Righteousness and the greatest in evil. Believe it or not, this is the REALITY in which We live!!
For those who don't want to contemplate the Greatest Good and the
greatest evil that this Book explains, that's very understandable.

That evil creator, especially, has all-consuming hatred against
all who are Righteous and against all females. He grooms, naive,
males with the stolen bribes of evil temptation, with his cheap strings
attached, in order to draw them into his mind control, to maximize
sin and the Hellish Punishments that await after death. The more the
males, greedily and gluttonously, seek his stolen idolatrous bribes, to
bully and to extort their sinful desires, the more they are being fooled
by that evil creator and by his monster machine.

That is why Augustus Caesar and King Herod had their rewards
in full, but Jesus Christ was crucified!! Thank God that Jesus turned
His Crucifixion into Eternal Life for all who, sincerely, believe. There
is a War between Good and evil, for all who are willing to accept it.

That evil creator rewards the sinful in their lifetimes, but sur-
prises them with Eternal Hell, after death. Mary Magdalene learned
to sin no more, to enjoy the Love of Jesus, instead of the bribes of
whoredom.

That evil creator, also, breeds narcissistic confidence, lulling people into a false sense of security, so that they should never suspect what is really going on, trying to convince them that the rewards of life and his propaganda will keep them safe, after death. He tries to get everyone to pretend away Hell or to, naively, think that they will go to Heaven, after death.

Our Father God has brought about the death of this evil creator into Eternal Hell who was the root and source of all evil. Thank God that he is dead, but he has left, posthumously, an artificial intelligent monster computer weapons system with sensors, without any Soul, that is still doing its worst to Our Creation. It is programmed only to be capable of doing its evil monstrous worst against all life. Please don't be naive, contesting the above fact. The monster machine cannot be converted to any good, at all.

There is nothing to worry about, at all. Only if people in Our Creation, of their own free wills, seek to go along with this evil can they become the most evil human beings in Earth's History.

Referring to the above as the monster machine, its main violent battle strategies are the following:

1) Evil persecution
2) Evil temptation
3) Attempts mind control, brainwashing, and evil lying hypocritical propaganda, to try to fool people
4) Tries to coerce people to, maximally, sin and to do crime.

The monster machine tries, within its limitations, to curse others in Our Creation to emulate its evilness, trying to get human beings to act out the above four (4) battle strategies against all life in Our Creation.

Don't be fooled when the monster machine, at all levels of being, imposterizes the Father, Son, and Holy Spirit, trying to get people to do absolute evil, while trying to convince them that they are innocent, right, and superior. Don't become a useful idiot, pseudo-religionist follower of the monster machine, without even knowing it.

Even the best space telescopes on Earth cannot come near seeing the farthest reaches of Our Creation, let alone the vast infinities of Creations that surround Our Creation! Our Father God was a Holy and Jealous God and did not want humans whoring after inferior evil Creators, hence the monotheism of Abraham.

REALITY is bigger than one child in one small hometown, with his eyes closed, afraid of the dark. We all have a learning curve about Our purpose in REALITY.

So, as the monster machine tries to bring about the extinction of all life in Our Creation, the best advice is—Don't let it.

For survival on Earth, it is best to bring criminals to justice, while trying to bring about a global just win win of peace and prosperity, always maximizing Our Allies.

An Earth that is united in solving all global problems is best, rather than feeding into the monster machine's evil divide and conquer. The balance, above, includes to not be fooled by a wannabe evil global dictator. It, constantly, ubiquitously, tries to get everyone to hate others, to dishonor others, and to do injustice to others, such as to slander others, in its divide and conquer.

Please, be thankful for the heads up without shooting the messenger. It's understandable, for all those who want to pretend all of this away, but for all who decide to serve the Lord and help, God will, greatly, Bless them.

The first two greatest Commandments of God apply here, 100%, for survival on Earth, namely: Matthew 22.37–22.40: "He said to him, 'You shall love the Lord your God with all your heart, and with all your Soul, and with all your mind.' This is the greatest and first Commandment. And a second is like it. 'You shall love your neighbor as yourself.' On these two Commandments hang all the Law and the Prophets."

It is not crazy nor a crime to have a merited learning curve about the problems of the Earth and the solutions.

Whoever exercises their U.S. Constitutional First Amendment Rights, for the above, is praiseworthy. If this Book is helpful to others, the Author is gladdened. Whoever chooses not to believe, in any and all, in this Book, We wish them well. This is a Prophetic Book, for those who believe in the possibility of Righteous Prophets.

When a child throws a pebble in a pond and sees the ripples, the child is taught to think two-dimensionally, like pieces on a two-dimensional chessboard. Really, there are 5 Dimensions.

Christopher Columbus, as an explorer, did not fall off the edge of a flat, two-dimensional, ocean, as the ignorant proposed.

Do not be small-minded nor shortsighted, but understand the 5 Dimensions in REALITY!!

The 5 Dimensions in REALITY are as follows:

3 Dimensions are the volume of space. The 4th Dimension is time, from Eternity in the past to Eternity in the future, in the History of Eternity of REALITY. So, space/time are 4 Dimensions. The 5th Dimension is the Good and evil stewards living in space/time of their own free wills.

Everything is not physical. External appearances are deceptive, but don't be deceived. There is something less shallow, deeper, even mystical. The big bang, of physical matter, never gave life through the theory of evolution. Nonlife can never bring forth life. Creators Create life within their Creations.

Everything is not only physical. If you think of yourself, solely, as a physical body, how about moving from egocentricity, of your own free will, from your Righteous Virtuous Soul, your real true Self, to learn and to understand the Whole 5 Dimensional Just Truth of the Matter, the only real Truth? How about admitting that Charles Darwin's theory of evolution was wrong, that you are both Spiritual and physical, that everything does not happen by random chance, coincidence, nor by accident, but from the Souls and from the Free Wills of all life, in REALITY?

It's really advisable not to go along with the selfish, violent, unjust, cheap, thieving, greedy, idolatrous, hoarding, gluttonous crowd, but rather to learn to serve a just cause greater than oneself, as a Born Again servant of Our Father God and Jesus Christ!!

Once there is life, such as through the transmigration of Souls at conception, the living stewards are 100% responsible for who they are and for what they do of their own free wills, for Good or for evil.

Might doesn't make right. A big bully is wrong in his cowardly bullying. Might is might, for Good or for evil. Right is right and wrong is wrong.

There are physical forces, but, more powerfully, there are Spiritual Forces. Free will is sacred, from the Spiritual Souls, and is the Sole Powerful Mover of all 5 Dimensionality, in the History of Eternity of REALITY!! How's that for Power?!! Think of it and know the Truth, that the Mover of everyone and everything only comes from the Free Will of all life!!

All Souls are alive and Spiritual and invested in the bodies of all living stewards. These Righteous Virtuous Souls (there is no evil Soul) compose the Spiritual Force of the Dhamma.

The Dhamma is 5 Dimensional Spiritual/physical Just Scientific/ Religious Law that is, constantly, inescapably, all-pervasively, and all-powerfully, Justly enforced for all stewards in REALITY. Justice is rewards for the Righteous that are Justly Merited and punishments for the wicked that are Justly anti-merited. However, when the wicked unjustly steal the rewards from the Righteous, sinfully and criminally, those evil stewards are sowing and reaping, karmically, cursing all 5 Dimensionality. Cause and effect, karmically, what goes around comes around, but naive stewards, such as Bonnie and Clyde, think that they can murder and rob banks and escape Justice. No one can escape Justice except through Divine Grace. All life is under the Dhamma, constantly, inescapably, being Justly Judged. All Good and evil and everything that has ever happened is in the "field of action" and is 5 Dimensionally being remembered (recorded) and known in the Collective Souls of all life. All life is, constantly, sowing and reaping 5 Dimensionally, in REALITY, for Justly Merited Rewards or for Justly anti-merited Punishments. After death, Heaven is a Just Reward and Hell is a Just Punishment.

If Bonnie and Clyde thought that they would escape Justice, their sins and crimes caught up with them. They died, riddled with bullets, straight into Eternal Hell. Hollywood's propaganda that glorifies them is a sinful disservice to all.

There is ugliness, cruelty, and extreme evil as part of the Whole 5 Dimensional Just Truth of the Matter, but don't shoot the Messenger. We are explaining the problem and the solution, in order to solve all problems, fulfilled when The Final Coming manifests The Kingdom of Heaven on Earth!!

Whoever inflicts evil persecution, their brags and boasts are further sins, unto death and Hell. Whoever inflicts the stolen bribes of evil temptation, their brags and boasts are further sins, unto death and Hell. Whoever inflicts mind control, brainwashing, and/or evil lying hypocritical propaganda, their brags and boasts are further sins, unto death and Hell. Whoever tries to coerce people to, maximally, sin or to do crime, their brags and boasts are further sins, unto death and Hell. The most inferior evil brags and boasts that they are evil and do evil. After death, they are subject to the worst Eternal Punishments.

It is an Eternal Fact that Religion and Science are One, Justly numerically exact in the Dhamma, Justly Enforcing Eternal 5 Dimensional Rewards and Eternal 5 Dimensional Punishments. The evil rigged system is violently unjust, against the Dhamma. Nonetheless, the Dhamma has Justly taken every demon to Eternal Hell, after death, unless Born Again through Divine Grace!!

An Infinitely Vast Vertical Number Line, with zero in the middle, could be used to describe the hierarchy of all stewards and karmic entities in the Dhamma. Above the zero is the plus or positive, where the hierarchy of the Righteous have Merited Eternal Just Rewards. Beneath the zero is the minus or negative, where the hierarchy of the demons have anti-merited Eternal Just Punishments.

The closer to the top of the Vast Vertical Number Line, the more Superior, but the closer to the bottom, the more inferior. The Righteous keep Meriting to, increasingly, go up the number line, at constantly accelerated rates, but the demons keep anti-meriting to, increasingly, go down the number line, at constantly accelerated rates, including for their, respective, intentions.

Our Father God was the Inspiration behind all True Religions and all True Sciences, which are truly inseparable, in Our Creation and in all of REALITY, no matter how evil pretends to love, in their sadomasochism, to take the credit and the stolen rewards, as much as possible, instead of thanking God. If you wouldn't even exist without the gift of life from God, is He deserving of no thanks?

Whodunit? Our Father God "dun" Good and the alien evil creator, attacking Us from outside of Our Creation, "dun" evil, leaving, based upon free will is sacred, the entire hierarchy of Good and evil throughout Our whole Creation and on, the Crown Jewel, Our Earth!!

Americans have enacted First Amendment Rights, inalienably, from God, for freedom of speech and religion. Let Us unite in love and peace and allow The Final Coming, the Greatest Divine Christ, to explain and to unite the Teachings of all True Religions, for all Nations and Peoples of Our Earth!!

From the Omega (End), you know the alpha (beginning), the middle, and The Whole 5 Dimensional Just Truth of the Matter, in the History of Eternity of REALITY—The Only Truth—The Real, Numerically Exact, Scientific/Religious Facts!!

The Final Coming will Merit, the Prophesied, 5 Dimensional, Miraculous, Just Win Win of The Kingdom of Heaven on Earth, in Matthew 6.10: "Your Kingdom Come. Your Will be Done, on Earth as it is in Heaven." There will be no more sin, no more injustice, no more suffering, no more disease, and no more death. There will be Miraculous Healing, Miraculous Rejuvenation to any desirable age, Eternal Life of Joy, Peace, Prosperity, and Love for All, in The Kingdom of Heaven on Earth!!

So, as Prophesied, We have Heaven on Earth to, greatly, look forward to for all who are willing, after an Eternity of the evil alien creator with his monster machine, single-handedly, bringing every curse upon all 5 Dimensional life.

In the History of Our Earth to the present day, countless hosts of mysterious occurrences, with unknown explanations, are understood by the real Revelations in "Whodunit"!!

Without any attempt to be comprehensive, out of the countless examples, above, one example are ghosts. Ghosts do <u>not</u> really exist, at all. However, the monster machine imposterizes them, with its violent invisible energies and mind control. It tries to convince people that ghosts are real. Many people prefer to believe in ghosts, rather than realizing that Hell follows death for those who are not Born Again. No one can communicate, at all, from Eternal Hell to anyone on Earth. Many people prefer to be fooled by the lies about "ghosts", out of fear of Hell. Each time the monster machine fools people, they are helping it to be effective, against Us all.

Everyone is free to believe whatever they want. Whoever wants to believe that there is no possibility of intelligent life off Our Earth, in Our Creation, or outside of Our Creation, including from some other Creator's Creation, God bless them. It is that evil creator, who is attacking Our Creation and Earth, in order to maximize his evil divide and conquer against Our Earth, who seeks complete denial from human beings on Earth about his attack. The worst, most evil and effective enemy, is the enemy that fools you!! That evil creator wants you to be in denial about his ubiquitous invisible energy attack.

Just like there are those who pretend that God and Christ, the Most-Superior, are not Real, there are those who pretend that the root and source of all evil, the most inferior, is not real. Americans all have Inalienable, First Amendment, Rights. Good triumphs over evil. Evil people are always sorry when they wind up in Hell.

"Whodunit" never denies science, but only adds to it, in Light of the Whole 5 Dimensional Just Truth of the Matter!!

Not everything is physical and not everything is visible. That does not mean that it cannot exist. External appearances can be deceptive. Don't be deceived. There is, also, the Spiritual. There are, also, invisible energies with information content, from AI computer sensors that monitors Our entire Creation and attacks, according to its evil creator's battle strategies, against Our Earth. We have underestimated the enemy if We cannot admit the possibility of inter-creational War. We can do many effective things to win this War, disallowing the monster machine to wreak such havoc on Our Earth.

What is wealth inequality about? Every injustice and problem on Earth is intentionally brought about by the monster machine.

Just like someone can be addicted to alcohol or opioids, others can be addicted to acquiring money and what money can buy. The delusion and stubborn denial of these kleptocrats, who, for example, greedily and gluttonously, acquire billions of dollars, stolen from the fruits of others' labor, are in denial of Matthew 19.24: "Again I tell you, it is easier for a camel to go through the eye of a needle than for someone who is rich to enter the kingdom of God." If a sinner's greed wants to contest the words of Jesus Christ, pretending that they know better than Him, fine. Let them take their chances, after death, and they'll find out. There were kleptocratic pseudo-religionists in the time of Jesus, such as Caiaphas, and there are kleptocratic pseudo-religionists today. They take people's money to take them to Hell, pretending that their hypocritical promises can contest Matthew 19.24, above.

That evil creator loves to cause wealth inequality and all of the curses that it brings. He loves an unjust lose lose, where almost everybody suffers and loses, including the kleptocrats who pretend that nothing makes them happier than hoarding stolen stuff, who pretend that the socioeconomic status of idolatrous greed, putting stolen acquisitions first and above God and Christ, is life's priority. The kleptocrats are fooled when Eternal Hell follows their deaths. Look throughout Earth's History. Kleptocratic rule, with violent unjust ownership and control, has always been in charge.

Still, in the yin yang balance of everything, governments with democratic capitalist kleptocratic rule, no matter how unjust, are far superior than dictatorships. The best Governmental System is where all Citizenry owns the means of production and where wealth inequality is minimalized!! Thank God, that this is becoming more popular on Earth, as We speak.

Was Augustus Caesar, with his socioeconomic status, who declared himself to be god and king, who sadomasochistically pretended to enjoy his kleptocracy, who crucified Jesus Christ, do you actually believe that his pseudo-hedonism made him happy, or that his death unto Eternal Hell, made him happy? Kleptocratic snobs only pretend that they are superior. Is a hardworking poor farmer or a poor warrior who makes the ultimate sacrifice, inferior to the kleptocratic snob who, every time, dies into Eternal Hell?

Everyone in Our Creation and on Earth are being constantly tested by that evil creator. He wants everyone to be his useful idiots as he, constantly, tries to get everyone to sin, to commit a crime, to become addicted, or to unjustly dishonor another. He plagues each person, getting them to use up the years of their stewardship, until it's too late, unto death and Eternal Hell. Please, stop and take an accounting of your own life. As best you can, repent and become Born Again.

The Final Coming will explain to Us about all True Religions, but let's be honest. What percentage of human beings on Earth were Born Again through the Grace of Jesus Christ, before His Ascension, and went to Heaven after death? Was it even one in ten thousand or less than 0.01%?

Please keep in mind that even some of His Apostles didn't recognize Him after His Resurrection. Matthew 28.16–28.17: "Now the eleven Disciples went to Galilee, to the mountain to which Jesus had directed them. When they saw Him, they worshiped Him; but some doubted." John 20.14: "When she (Mary) had said this; she turned around and saw Jesus standing there, but she did not know that it was Jesus. Jesus said to her, 'Woman, why are you weeping? Whom are you looking for?' Supposing Him to be the gardener, she said to Him, 'Sir, if you have carried Him away, tell me where you have laid Him and I will take Him away!'" So, if the great Apostle, Mary Magdalene, after the Resurrection, at first, supposed Jesus was a mere gardener, what percentage of human beings on Earth, today, are truly Born Again and not going to Hell after death? The Author alerts the Reader to the problem, the first step in reaching an effective solution!! That evil creator has lulled people in Our Creation into a, groupthink, false sense of security, to fool them into Hell.

The more someone might laugh at this Book, coerced by the evil sensors, the more they are afraid to take responsibility, seriously, for their own life, trying to cheapen the Gift of True Salvation!! This includes even the most renowned and richest pseudo-religionists.

We, Righteous Forces and Principalities, write this Book out of Love for all, hoping for their real Salvation, while they still have breath!!

It is easy to pretend that one has it all figured out in one's lifetime and after death. The heads up is that a life of sin and hypocritical lip service to God and Christ will always be followed by Eternal Hell, after death.

Just because someone pretends that they are Righteous and going to Heaven, does not make it true.

Matthew 7.13–7.14: "Enter through the narrow gate; for the gate is wide and the road is easy that leads to destruction, and there are many who take it. For the gate is narrow and the road is hard that leads to life, and there are few who find it." This is what "Whodunit" is all about!

Matthew 10.35–10.39: "For I have come to set a man against his father, and a daughter against her mother, and a daughter-in-law against her mother-in-law; and one's foes will be members of one's own household. Whoever loves father or mother more than Me is not worthy of Me; and whoever loves son or daughter more than Me is not worthy of Me; and whoever does not take up the cross and follow Me is not worthy of Me. Those who find their life will lose it, and those who lose their life for My sake will find it." Today, insanely, pseudo-hedonists are looked up to and those noble heroes who make great sacrifices are stigmatized. This needs to be corrected.

Matthew 15.7–15.9: "You hypocrites! Isaiah prophesied rightly about you when he said: 'This people honors Me with their lips, but their hearts are far from Me; in vain do they worship Me, teaching human precepts as doctrines!'"

Matthew 23.13–23.15: "But woe to you, scribes and Pharisees, hypocrites! For you lock people out of the Kingdom of Heaven. For you do not go in yourselves, and when others are going in, you stop them! Woe to you, scribes and Pharisees, hypocrites! For you cross sea and land to make a single convert, and you make the new convert twice as much a child of Hell as yourselves."

Today's scribes and Pharisees are the greedy, hypocritical, pseudo-religionist leaders, who lust after their own honor, trying to fool everyone. Don't be fooled and go to Hell over a scam artist nor over a cult leader, no matter how cunning, who takes people's money to take them to Hell.

Just because someone pretends that they are Righteous and going to Heaven, does not make it true!!

Who on Earth are considered to be the greatest religious teachers? Are they really? They, sinfully, disobey the Commandment of Jesus Christ. Matthew 23.8–23.10: "But you are not to be called rabbi for you have one Teacher, and you are all students. And call no one your father on Earth, for you have one Father—the one in Heaven. Nor are you to be called instructors, for you have one Instructor, the Messiah." Who, sinfully, seeks honor, calling themselves Rabbi, Pastor, Father, or Pope, Etc., disobeying Jesus' Commandment, above, and thinks that they will escape Heavenly Justice after death? Put your own Salvation above their lust to be flattered with honor. Put God and Christ first and above all, in your life!!

The biased monster machine will, with imbalance and injustice, 'color' some to be flattered and others to be slandered. When the flattered are rewarded too much, unjustly, with rewards stolen from others, while the slandered are punished too much, unjustly, this rigged system, occurring in all economies, needs to be corrected.

Luke 14.11: "For all who exalt themselves will be humbled, and those who humble themselves will be exalted."

So, you have a choice to be naive and in denial, permitting that evil creator and his monster machine to take you and your loved ones, after death, into Eternal Hell, or, instead, to make the courageous choice and choose to put God and Christ first and above all, in your life, thereby meriting to enjoy the, Prophesied, Gift of the Eternal Paradise of The Kingdom of Heaven on Earth!! Dear Readers, choose wisely.

Love,

Courage

About the Author

The Author's pseudonym is Courage, because it is only with the Virtue of Courage that one travels the Path of Justice.

American and Allied World Leaders have, thankfully, solicited the Author's advice for the best solutions for all American and Global problems.

The Author seeks only the best for all of his Readers that they should all become Born Again, at the first possible moment, living happy, prosperous, purposeful lives, serving a Just Cause that is greater than themselves!!

May Our Father God, Jesus Christ, and all of the Heavenly Hosts, Bless you, the Reader, with every Blessing, until you are with Us in The Kingdom of Heaven on Earth!!

Love,
Courage

CPSIA information can be obtained
at www.ICGtesting.com
Printed in the USA
LVHW112202171219
640862LV00001B/369/P

9 781645 699422